This book is dedicated to all who find Nature not an adversary to conquer and destroy, but a storehouse of infinite knowledge and experience linking man to all things past and present. They know conserving the natural environment is essential to our future well-being.

MOUNT RAINIER
THE STORY BEHIND THE SCENERY®
by Ray "Skip" Snow

Ray "Skip" Snow is a career employee of the National Park Service. He has served as a park planner and environmental specialist at the agency's Denver Service Center, as an interpreter at Mount Rainier, and as a district naturalist at Theodore Roosevelt National Park in North Dakota. He graduated from Ohio's Miami University with undergraduate and graduate degrees in biological and environmental sciences. The years that Skip lived and worked in Mount Rainier National Park have given him a special appreciation of and admiration for the wonders of Mount Rainier and the Pacific Northwest.

Mount Rainier National Park, *located in southwestern Washington, established in 1899, preserves the greatest single-peak glacial system in the United States.*

Front cover: Mount Rainier from Reflection Lake, by Ed Cooper. Inside front cover: Henry M. Jackson Memorial Visitor Center at Paradise, by Ed Cooper. Title page: Avalanche Lilies, by Russ Grater.

Book Design by K. C. DenDooven, Edited by Peter C. Howorth

Third Printing, 1990

MOUNT RAINIER: THE STORY BEHIND THE SCENERY. © 1984 KC PUBLICATIONS, INC. LC 83-80764. ISBN 0-916122-83-2.

A mountain beyond imagining. A mountain unbelievable. Like fairy tale magic, an aura of myth, fable, and gods pervades. The splendor of altitude, the serenity of tall timber, the haunting presence of an explosive time gone by and yet to come are the vivid and abiding impressions given by Mount Rainier.

The altitude of Mount Rainier is so deceiving that our perceptions are continually challenged. In scale and distance the mountain subjects our minds and muscles to whimsical trickery. Features that seem close enough to touch remain in the distance even as we approach them.

But the grandest deceptions with which this sleeping monarch of Washington teases us are the untold violence of its birth and the unwritten cataclysm of its future. An observer who has the time can discover the haunting presence of awesome events gone by and glean a feeling for the harbinger of future fire.

Such a mountain must be seen to be fully appreciated, although this in itself can frustrate the most persistent explorer. Dense fog, wind, rain, and snow descend upon the summit without much warning—even in summer. The winter sightseer must typically contend with eight out of ten days with little or no clear sky. In fact, many travelers have headed home with hardly a glimpse of the cloud-hidden heights, although the rocks underfoot and the valleys below are as much a part of Mount Rainier as its ice-covered crest.

Understanding even a smattering of the intricacies and subtleties of this mountain reveals a rich universe and evokes our sense of wonder. Although legends and fables may color our experience, it is compelling and exciting to learn the true story. The real world of fire and ice can be just as bizarre and awesome as any make-believe.

Preceding pages by Art Wolfe /Aperture

The Mountain

It is no coincidence that Mount Rainier, today a dormant volcano, lies near 14 major volcanic peaks and a multitude of lesser volcanic features. The volcanoes of northwestern North America are part of the "Ring of Fire," made up of volcanic ranges that nearly surround the Pacific Ocean. This ring includes the Aleutians, the western coast of North and South America, Antarctica, eastern Indonesia, the Philippines, and Japan. The shattered Krakatoa, the astonishingly beautiful Fujiyama, and Mount Saint Helens are all found on this ring, which includes approximately three fourths of the world's active volcanoes. Over 400 volcanoes have been active on the Ring of Fire in recorded history.

This concentration of volcanic peaks can be explained by the theory of plate tectonics. According to this concept, the surface of the earth consists of seven or more huge, constantly moving plates that interact with one another. One type of volcanic eruption occurs when two plates come together, sometimes producing violent eruptions. This process has given rise to some of the most breathtaking scenery in the Pacific Northwest. In other areas of the Ring of Fire, different plate movements have resulted in other volcanic activities.

Mount Rainier originated where the oceanic Juan de Fuca plate collided with the North American continental plate, then plunged beneath it in a process known as *subduction*. This process continues even today, for the Juan de Fuca plate still moves about an inch a year in a northeasterly direction.

The rate of subduction may be partly responsible for the amount of volcanic activity in an area. Northwestern North America enjoys a comparatively quiet landscape, perhaps because the rate is slower than in other regions.

The subduction of the Juan de Fuca plate and others around the Pacific generates great earthquakes. Subduction may also provide molten rock and pressure to power volcanoes and thrust up mountains. Volcanoes form where cracks or faults in the earth's crust allow molten rock to expand and move toward the surface.

A volcano is defined as the vent through which material rises as well as the feature formed by material from the vent. Volcanoes built entirely of fire-broken rock or fragmented material are called cinder cones. These piles of large and small rocks are often steep and symmetrical.

When highly liquid lava, known as *basalt*, flows like a river from a vent, it can travel a con-siderable distance, forming a broad, low shape like an overturned dinner plate. Such forms are called shield volcanoes.

Mount Rainier is a composite volcano, built of lava flows and fragmented rock. Indeed, most scenic hallmarks of the Pacific Northwest, including Mount Adams, Mount Saint Helens, and Mount Hood, are composite volcanoes. Compared to cinder cones and shields, the composite volcanoes are steeper, higher, and often more explosive when they do erupt.

Mount Rainier and the Cascade Range did not exist some 50 million years ago. In their place was a broad lowland partly occupied by swamps, lakes, rivers, and marine inlets. Rivers spread sand and clay into these waters. The accumulated material, including decaying vegetation, was compacted into sandstone, shale, and coal. These rock layers, which can be seen today along the Mowich Lake Road northwest of the park, were pushed upward from their origin in shallow waters.

Numerous volcanic eruptions occurred in the lowland—some on land and some under water—spreading debris over vast areas. About 12 million years ago, masses of molten rock many miles wide moved through the older rocks, forming a beautiful salt-and-pepper-colored foundation of granodiorite for Mount Rainier. But the landscape gave little outward sign of the changes

Massive lava outpourings were responsible for most of the early building of Mount Rainier. Lava flowed repeatedly down deep canyons, cooling to form dark gray columns in some places. Because these ancient flows resisted erosion, most are now ridgetops.

RALPH A. CLEVENGER

occurring 40 miles beneath the surface: changes that would give rise to a monumental piece of topography.

About a million years ago, the country that now surrounds Mount Rainier probably looked quite similar to the way it does today. Volcanic rocks and sediment, rising above a broad lowland, had been crumpled, folded, broken, and uplifted, forming the nearby Cascade Range. Rivers ran swiftly, cutting through steep, forested valleys. The rugged Tatoosh Range, which now borders the southern flank of Mount Rainier, was probably as picturesque then as it is now.

More than likely, Mount Rainier announced its birth with a series of earthquakes of increasing frequency. At a weak spot in the earth's surface, a central vent tore open a fissure. Molten rock surged upward. Thick lava oozed from this vent and flowed as far as 15 miles down the ancient river valleys. These flows filled the deep canyons of the surrounding mountains and later resisted erosion by both rivers and glaciers. Streams cut new beds along the sides of the lava flows, leaving the once-molten rivers to form ridges like the spokes

JEFF GNASS

Massive and weather-beaten Mount Adams is the second highest peak in the Pacific Northwest. Like Mount Rainier, Mount Adams is a composite volcano. Steam and heavy sulphur deposits on its summit remind us that Mount Adams is not yet dead.

RALPH A. CLEVENGER

of a wheel. Rampart Ridge, Burroughs Mountain, Grand Park, and Klapatche Ridge are the remains of such lava flows.

Thinner and much shorter flows of lava followed as the volcano grew. These layers formed steep slopes, gradually increasing the mountain's height. About 75,000 years ago, Mount Rainier probably stood over 16,000 feet high.

Layers of pumice and of volcanic ash can often be seen in stream banks or along hillsides where trails have been cut. Mount Rainier did not deposit all these layers. Mount Mazama, the volcano that collapsed to create Crater Lake in Oregon, deposited a substantial amount over 6,800 years ago. Mount Saint Helens blanketed the slopes several times, including laying down a yellow sand-like seam of pumice as much as 20 inches

Pinnacle Peak is one of several making up the rugged Tatoosh Range. Formed by ancient volcanic ash flows that predate Mount Rainier, the Tatoosh Range is the southern end of a great U-shaped stratum underlying Mount Rainier.

thick on Mount Rainier's western slope more than 3,300 years ago. Mount Saint Helens's most recent addition has settled into the moss and among the decaying wood—a thin layer of slate-gray ash deposited in the spring of 1980.

When Mount Rainier erupted, stately firs were probably flattened or defoliated as a result of the blast. Streams were clogged with mud, grit, and volcanic dust. A scene of utter destruction may have prevailed, much like the aftermath of the Mount Saint Helens eruption.

Strangely enough, volcanoes, despite their destructive power, are considered benefactors. Volcanic rock, pumice, and ash are rich in minerals. They weather into fertile soil that now supports lush lowland vegetation, farmlands, and fields of subalpine wildflowers.

As lava flows diminished less than 10,000 years ago, Mount Rainier's cone was reduced by collapse and erosion. Any renewed construction was stripped away by numerous mudflows triggered by steam explosions and earthquakes. Mudflows are one of the most destructive of volcanic phenomena. Water from melted snow and ice combines with clay, silt, sand, volcanic ash, and cinders to carry boulders, trees, and other objects down the mountainsides. These mudflows, driven by gravity, can travel more than 60 miles an hour.

Some 5,800 years ago, a sudden collapse of Mount Rainier's 16,000-foot summit sent a mudflow containing over half a cubic mile of material thundering down the White River Valley. This wall of mud, nearly 100 feet high, buried 125 square miles, including the area where the cities of Kent, Sumner, Auburn, and Puyallup are now

Mount Rainier is eroded by the large-scale movement of glacial material and by catastrophic mudflows, combined with the localized effects of frost heave and silt washed away by rain and melting snow.

located. It finally stopped beneath the waters of Puget Sound. Known as the Osceola mudflow, it is one of the largest ever discovered.

All of Mount Rainier's valleys may have been scoured by mudflows at one time or another. Even the now-serene and aptly named Paradise was not immune. Between 5,800 and 6,600 years ago, a slurry of rock and mud some 600 feet thick inundated Paradise Valley after sweeping down

These ash-covered snowbanks mark the recent eruption of nearby Mount Saint Helens. Layers of pumice and ash from other volcanic eruptions can often be seen in hillside cuts and in streambanks.

Fireweed commonly grows in areas disturbed by natural catastrophes. Its pink blossoms became a common sight soon after the eruption of Mount Saint Helens.

the Nisqually Glacier. To the west another mudflow temporarily submerged Round Pass to a depth of 400 feet, flooding the South Puyallup River and Tahoma Creek valleys. This was a particularly dramatic event because Round Pass is more than 600 feet above the valley floor.

Mount Rainier began another series of eruptions between 2,000 and 2,500 years ago. At some time during these eruptions, an avalanche of ash, globs of airborne lava, and rock with a temperature of 600 degrees Fahrenheit buried the South Puyallup River valley floor. The rocks cooled, later coming to resemble the cracked crust of a loaf of bread. "Breadcrust bombs," as these rocks are called, may be seen on the West Side Road.

Mount Rainier's eastern crater rim is kept partially free of snow by heat and steam from within the mountain. The snow-filled crater contains roughly the equivalent of a billion gallons of water.

These eruptions ended with the building of the present summit cone about 2,000 years ago. This cone consists of thin layers of black andesitic lava. The top is crowned with two overlapping craters, the larger one about a quarter of a mile across. The point where these craters overlap marks the mountain's highest point, known as Columbia Crest (14,410 feet). Two lesser summits on the sides, Liberty Cap (14,112 feet) and Point Success (14,158 feet), are remnants of an older, once higher, cone.

RIVERS OF ICE

Mount Rainier, as well as the other major composite volcanoes of the Pacific Northwest, was born during the Ice Age. This period, known as the Pleistocene, began 2 million to 3 million years ago and ended some 10,000 years ago. During this time the world's climate showed cyclic increases in snowfall and cooler weather.

As more winter snow fell than could melt in the cool summers, snow built up on the land. Air was squeezed from the accumulating snow pack, changing the snow into ice. Enormous sheets of ice, driven by gravity, crept across the land and down river valleys. At one point during the Ice Age the site of Seattle was beneath 4,000 feet of ice. Glaciers gouged and sculptured much of the continental landscape, using rocks and boulders as abrasives.

These abrasives were quarried out by the glaciers themselves. Scientists believe that cracks in the underlying rock, formed prior to glaciation, were filled with water that froze and expanded, prying up large blocks of rock. As the glaciers moved over these blocks, they forced the loosened rock from its place. Once incorporated into the glacial ice, these blocks were used to scrape and pluck other abrasive materials. As a result, the underlying rock was ground down and each glacier cut its own trench.

Mount Rainier's great height, towering into the cooler reaches of the atmosphere, allowed

The Nisqually Glacier and the Wilson, a small tributary glacier, span more than two square miles. At its thickest point, the Nisqually is about 330 feet deep. Its immense weight, aided by gravity, pulls the ice mass downward. When such a glacier enters a V-shaped river valley, it broadens the walls of the valley. As a result, the valley becomes U-shaped: wider, deeper, and straighter, with steep sides and a rounded bottom. The Nisqually Valley is a typical glacier-scoured canyon.

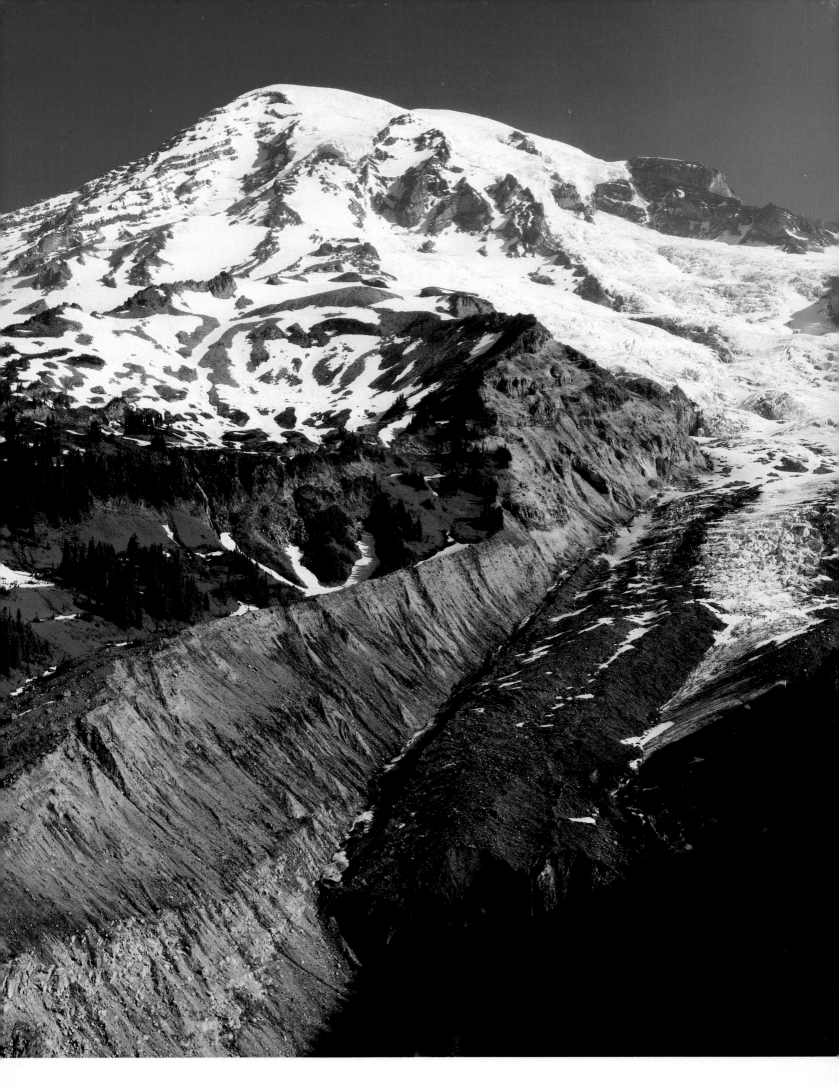

The Emmons Glacier, on the northeastern slope of Mount Rainier, is the largest in the contiguous United States. It was named after the world-renowned nineteenth-century geologist, Samuel Emmons.

it to support numerous glaciers during most of its formative years. Even before the mountain reached its greatest elevation, and as molten rock issued from its vents, glaciers were cutting deep U-shaped valleys and huge bowl-shaped arenas, called *cirques*, into the slopes. A succession of lava flows contributed to this erosion, partly or entirely melting many of the glaciers, thus unleashing tremendous floods. During the last major glacial period, which ended 10,000 years ago, the glaciers of Mount Rainier grew to be as much as 40 miles in length.

As the climate warmed between 4,000 and 8,000 years ago, however, the glaciers of Mount Rainier receded. They began to advance again about 3,500 years ago during what is sometimes called the "Little Ice Age." Today's glaciers are considerably smaller than they were only 60 years ago. Since the 1950s the glaciers have remained relatively stable or have advanced.

Mount Rainier now supports over 35 square miles of ice, including 26 officially named glaciers and numerous unnamed ice fields. Mount Rainier boasts the largest single-peak glacier system

The Carbon Glacier on the north side of Mount Rainier, blackened by morainal debris, has made small advances in the last 20 years. Each glacier has developed a distinct personality with varieties of ice falls, rock, and crevasses.

in the contiguous 48 states. Like streamers from a maypole, six of these glaciers radiate from the summit.

The condition of these glaciers has been of concern to the people of the Northwest for some time. The glaciers provide a constant supply of fresh water for domestic use, irrigation, and the generation of hydroelectric power. Because of their importance, we know a great deal about Mount Rainier's rivers of ice.

Mount Rainier is made of unstable fragmented rock and offers little resistance to the erosive power of glaciers. Underlying this fragmented rock is harder, more resistant bedrock that is grooved and polished by the movement of glaciers.

As glaciers quarry rock from the mountainside, they transport and deposit material into piles, or *moraines*. These ridges of rock form along the sides of a glacier and along the ice front, known as the *terminus*. A glacier deposits most of its debris at the terminus. Consequently, the leading edge of a glacier is an extremely dangerous

Strewn with debris, a blackened glacier, actively eroding, transports and deposits large quantities of material.

Silent sentries, ice pinnacles more than 50 feet tall appear and disappear with the movement of glaciers.

KEITH GUNNAR

13

place to explore, for rocks fall almost constantly from the melting ice. In addition to plucking rocks out and piling them into moraines, glacial ice also grinds rock into a fine powder.

Debris ranging from flourlike particles to large boulders is carried away by turbulent meltwater streams flowing from tunnels beneath every glacier. How turbid the water is roughly indicates how active a glacier is. The Nisqually River, fed by the active Nisqually Glacier, is heavily laden with silt in summer. Glaciers like the Paradise, which move very slowly or not at all and therefore do little work, produce clear streams like the Paradise River.

Downstream, as the steepness of the valley floor decreases, meltwater streams lose their ability to carry larger rocks and cobbles. The "glacial flour," a finer material, remains suspended, to be deposited in lakes and marine inlets as much as 40 miles away from its source on Mount Rainier.

When sections of ice within a glacier move at different speeds or the ice flow passes over broken terrain, the stress causes the ice to separate. Large cracks called *crevasses* form. These are the most awesome features of the glaciers. Splits over 100 feet deep exist, often bathed in an eerie blue light.

Labyrinths of crevasses, opening and closing from year to year and weakly bridged by snow, are a constant hazard to mountaineers. Enormous blocks of ice and towering pinnacles referred to as *seracs* also make the going difficult, even though it looks easy from a distance.

Some parts of the glaciers can be readily visited. The popular Paradise and Stevens glaciers can be reached by a three-mile trail from the Paradise Visitor Center. The lower portions of the glaciers are relatively flat and inactive. Here, small streams of meltwater have helped carve out caves in the ice. They are not always accessible, however. Should the previous winter's snowfall be heavy and the summer cool, the ice caves may remain buried even in summer.

Under the right conditions sunlight filters through the ice, bathing the caves in an iridescent blue glow. Inside, visitors can see where ice has plucked rocks from the stream bed to use as tools for sculpturing the mountain. Over four

Dwarfed by a world of perpetual snow and ice, a climber challenges a crevasse on the Ingraham Glacier. Some crevasses are over 100 feet deep.

miles of tunnels were revealed when the caves were mapped in 1973, but in 1981 the caves were only a mile and a half long. In the last few years huge sections of the ceilings have collapsed because of decreasing snowfall and warmer temperatures, resulting in an ice trench rather than a cave. Such conditions can be hazardous to visitors.

Even though some parts of the glaciers are melting, snow from Pacific storms continues to add to the glaciers in record accumulations. The mountain intercepts moisture-laden air flowing inland from the ocean. Pushed around and over Mount Rainier, this air cools, dropping most of its moisture as rain or snow on the western slope. Consequently, the north and east slopes of the mountain receive less precipitation, making days at Sunrise often warmer and dryer than at Paradise.

RAY ATKESON

Strongly tied to yearly weather patterns, the Paradise Ice Caves were once extensive and easily reached. Recently, however, the caverns have become reduced in size or have even become inaccessible.

The heaviest snowfalls occur at between 5,000 and 10,000 feet. Higher up, the snowfall actually diminishes; what does fall is often blown away by high winds. Accumulations at 9,000 feet and above probably add mass to the glaciers, while snow at lower elevations does not survive the summer sun.

Paradise holds the world's record for the largest accumulated snowfall in a year. The record

was set in the winter of 1971-1972 when 1,122 inches of snow fell. During some winters it is possible to stand at the top of the 23-foot weather tower without climbing the pole!

The mass of ice on the summit creates cloud caps that often conceal the upper part of the mountain. Warm, moist air meets cool air over the ice, causing the water vapor to condense into clouds of fog or ice shaped like the side view of a lens, hence the meteorological term, *lenticular* clouds. So unusual and distinctive is their shape that lenticular clouds have been mistaken for UFOs. These clouds, which form on the windward side of the summit and dissipate on the lee slope, often are accompanied by winds of more than 50 miles an hour. They can signify an approaching storm.

RECENT ACTIVITY

Since the settlement of the Pacific Northwest in the 1800s, Mount Rainier has served notice on several occasions that its volcanic fires are not extinguished. The most recent eruptions, marked by a layer of pumice, occurred between 1820 and 1894. Based upon the reports of casual observers and newspaper articles, Mount Rainier may have erupted as many as 14 times during this period.

In December of 1963 millions of cubic yards of volcanic rock peeled in quick succession from

ED COOPER

the north face of Little Tahoma Peak onto the Emmons Glacier, perhaps because of a steam explosion rather than an actual eruption. The shower of rock shattered into fragments and avalanched down the ice, becoming airborne at the glacier's terminus. The material traveled about four miles before coming to rest within a half mile of White River Campground. Among the dust and rock fragments were boulders as large as railroad cars.

Subtle reminders of the mountain's volcanic origins are more numerous. These range from the unpleasant smell of hydrogen sulfide gas and localized steam jets to small explosions and mysterious melt depressions on the upper part of the mountain. In 1961 an explosion ripped open a hole near Gibraltar Rock, showering the Cowlitz Glacier with debris.

The two summit craters are now filled with

snow and ice, but within them lies a constant reminder of new beginnings. Volcanic heat issuing from beneath the packed snow has melted a system of tunnels and caves totaling a mile and a half in length. Mount Rainier is thought to share this feature with only Mount Baker, to the north, and Mount Wrangell in Alaska. Included in the ice maze is a pool of meltwater which was 18 feet deep in 1972, the only time it was measured. Its temperature hovers around freezing.

TOMORROW

The potential dangers of Mount Rainier and other Cascade volcanoes prompted scientists to begin a volcano watch in the 1960s. A number of procedures were used to monitor the mountain. Infrared or heat-recording photographs of Mount Rainier's summit were taken. Comparing photos taken over a period of time revealed whether the hot spots were increasing, decreasing, or shifting.

Earthquake monitoring stations (seismographs) were installed to record local and distant tremors. (An exhibit describing seismographs can be seen at the Jackson visitor center.) In 1980 Mount Saint Helens clearly demonstrated that certain kinds of earthquakes, known as harmonic tremors, can accompany the underground movement of molten rock that may sometimes precede an eruption. Even though the eruption of Mount Saint Helens provided invaluable information, the science of volcanic prediction is still too new to be reliable.

As early as 1973 Dwight Crandell, a U.S. Geological Survey geologist, recognized the need to plan for volcanic eruptions and published a map entitled "Potential Hazards from Future Erup-

JOEL MUR

The Willis Wall, named for the geologist Bailey Willis, rises 4,000 feet above the Carbon Glacier in an incline of fragmented rock impregnated with ice. The ice cap on the summit, exposing a 300-foot-thick wall of ice, overhangs the Willis Wall and is the source of some of the largest avalanches on Mount Rainier.

For many years the U.S. Geological Survey has studied the annual and long-term changes in the glacial systems of North America. Measurements taken of the Nisqually Glacier are part of this monitoring program.

tions of Mount Rainier, Washington." This map showed what might happen if Mount Rainier were to erupt again, including which areas would be affected by flood, mudflow, lava, and ash fall. But the map was based on the past; the intensity of Mount Rainier's next eruption could be more devastating than we can imagine.

Prior to the eruption of Mount Saint Helens, volcanic hazard maps provided colorful wall displays and interesting reading. Afterward, with 36 people killed and 21 missing and over a billion dollars' worth of property damaged, such maps took on new meaning. They now provide hints and possible plans for survival. Mount Rainier and the other Cascade volcanoes must be viewed as brooding threats as well as "the silent guardians" of the Northwest.

SUGGESTED READING

CRANDELL, DWIGHT R. *The Geologic Story of Mount Rainier.* Washington, D.C.: U.S. Geological Survey, 1973.

CRANDELL, DWIGHT R. *Map Showing Potential Hazards from Future Eruptions of Mount Rainier, Washington.* Washington, D.C.: U.S. Geological Survey, 1973.

DECKER, ROBERT, and BARBARA DECKER. *Volcanoes.* San Francisco: W. H. Freeman, 1981.

HARRIS, STEPHEN L. *Fire Mountains of the West.* Missoula, Montana: Mountain Press Publishing Company, 1988.

JEROME, JOHN. *On Mountains: Thinking About Terrain.* New York: McGraw Hill Book Company, 1978.

MACDONALD, GORDON. *Volcanoes.* Englewood Cliffs, N.J.: Prentice-Hall Incorporated, 1972.

MCKEE, BATES. *Cascadia: The Geologic Evolution of the Pacific Northwest.* New York: McGraw Hill Book Company, 1972.

U.S. Geological Survey. *Map of the Nisqually Glacier, Mount Rainier National Park.* Washington, D.C.: U.S. Geological Survey, 1976.

The eruption of Mount Saint Helens on May 18, 1980, was indeed impressive. It was the first volcanic eruption in the contiguous United States since the milder eruptions of Lassen Peak, California, which occurred from 1914 to 1917. Mount Rainier, like Mount Saint Helens, is a sleeping giant, but by no means a dead one. Should Mount Rainier erupt again, mudflows rather than explosions of ash would pose the greatest potential for wholesale destruction—and Mount Rainier has a history of producing massive mudflows. Some 5,800 years ago Mount Rainier's 16,000-foot summit collapsed. The resultant Osceola Mudflow, a veritable avalanche of debris, covered about 125 square miles with a layer of mud and rock. The flow stopped just short of the present site of Tacoma, some 65 miles away. By comparison, the volume of mud deposited downstream by Mount Saint Helens was about one twentieth that of the ancient Osceola Mudflow. Even so, 1980 mudflows were responsible for flooding and destruction, bringing shipping on the Columbia River to a halt.

Mount Saint Helens
May 18, 1980

Mount Saint Helens was the most perfect composite cone in the Pacific Northwest before it erupted. Because of its great height, Mount Rainier probably always supported glaciers that continue to erode its countenance. As a result, it is unlikely that Mount Rainier ever exhibited a perfect composite cone shape.

The eruption of Mount Saint Helens was triggered by the collapse of the north flank, which caused a tremendous landslide. The blast that reduced the mountain's stature was partially directed northeast, devastating 150 square miles. A new dome is forming in the crater as the mountain rebuilds itself.

PHOTOS BY RAY ATKESON

Forests and Fields

The roots of a towering fir or an inch-high tuft of alpine buckwheat weave part of the fibers of a carpet that must contend with erosion and eruption. Despite the power of avalanches, rock slides, mudflows, and explosions, the plant communities somehow endure.

The breadth, diversity, and age of these plant communities convey an impression of permanence, but the recent eruption of Mount Saint Helens reminds us that tall timber has no corner on permanency. In a matter of minutes towering forests up to 17 miles from the volcano were leveled or they simply disappeared. More than 200 square miles of forests were gone. They will return, probably only to disappear again. Assaulted by fire and ice, the forests of the Cascades have come and gone many times. Their story is one of resilience.

The lush overmantle of Mount Rainier contrasts with the heavily logged areas bordering the park. Our demand for cleared land for roads, buildings, and crops, as well as for lumber and wood products, has certainly taken its toll of plant communities elsewhere. But at Mount Rainier the luxuriance of the native plant life is a tribute to its triumph over natural competition, the elements, and the mountain.

Towering above the Pacific, Mount Rainier appears divided into a land of trees and no trees. A closer look will show a rich world divided into orderly groups of living organisms, much like neighborhoods, called life zones. To travel these life zones from the mountain's base to its summit is similar to experiencing the landscapes between Seattle and the Arctic Circle.

THE LOWLAND FOREST

Mount Rainier's lowland forests contain evergreens—like those in the Grove of the Patriarchs in the park's southeast corner—which rival the redwoods of California. Old-growth Douglas fir, western red cedar, and western hemlock appear in majestic stands along the roadside. Some trees may tower more than 200 feet, with diameters in excess of 8 feet. These slow-maturing trees live 500 years or more.

Rainfall is heaviest in the far northwest corner of the park. At Carbon River, named for the thin coal deposits found in the area, the lowland forest is at its best. Here, a nature trail winds through what some botanists claim is part of a temperate rain forest.

The temperate rain forest, largely a coastal

ED COOPER

A combination of rain and snow results in an annual precipitation of about 80 inches on the southwest side of Mount Rainier, supporting a legion of greenery.

Subalpine flower fields come to life by mid-June. By July, as many as 40 species may be in bloom.

phenomenon, is identified by the presence of Sitka spruce, heavy rainfall, summer fogs, nurse logs (fallen trees that nurture new plants), and an abundance of mosses and ferns. The temperate rain forest of Carbon River is notable because it is so far inland.

Very little sunlight reaches the floor of the lowland forest because the upper reaches of fir and cedar come together in a dense emerald canopy. This provides favorable conditions for the shade-tolerant western hemlock, whose seedlings quickly sprout and overtake the sun-loving species. If hemlock were left undisturbed by fire or mudflow, it would soon dominate the forest. Beneath this green cathedral flourishes a lush understory of smaller plants. Over 35 species of flowers live in the deep shade.

Nonflowering mosses and liverworts live beneath this world. The task of fertilization in this miniature forest is facilitated by the rain and dampness of the forest floor. Sperm swim through the water to eggs. These diminutive plants, with their primitive reproductive systems, harken to a time when jungles of tree-sized mosses and ferns teemed in a world dominated by non-flowering plants.

After the warm rains of early fall, the fruiting bodies, commonly called mushrooms, of over 150 species of fungi spring from threadlike subterranean masses known as *mycelia*. These mushrooms accent the forest floor with a full range of colors, sizes, shapes, and odors. They are decorated with scales, curls, veils, and slime. Some are deadly poisonous, while others are gastronomic joys. Their main purpose is to break down organic material, thus fertilizing the soil. They obtain their food from living plants or animals or from their remains after they die.

Whatever their origin, the forest dead are the wellsprings of new life. The bleached or charred skeleton of a Douglas fir provides perches and homes for flycatchers, hawks, owls, and pileated woodpeckers. Bats and small rodents find shelter in the folds of peeling bark. Dying trees, no longer able to resist attacks by insects, become good hunting grounds for a host of insect-eating animals. The size and complexity of the forest insect community is impressive. In one study over 300 species of insects were found to inhabit a single dead Douglas fir.

The floor of the lowland forest is a jackstraw arrangement of fallen snags brought down by wind. All are in various stages of rot. These logs, richer in nutrients and with better drainage than the surrounding soil, become nurse logs—beds for thousands of seedlings, especially western hemlock. These spongelike logs provide water to both plants and animals during droughts.

Black-tailed deer, pine martens, and field mice are among the many animals that use this maze of downed trees as a convenient series of trails. These mammals can move about free of the rocks, brush, and snarled roots of the forest floor in much the same way we use freeways.

Porcupines and snowshoe hares make their homes amidst the dense mass of lowland timber and underbrush. Several species of garter snakes and the secretive rubber boa work their way through the tangled vegetation. Six-inch banana

KEITH GUNNAR

This skunk cabbage will soon sport huge leaves to catch filtered sunlight.

Seldom seen, the rubber boa feeds on small mammals.

TOM & PAT LEESON

slugs, covered entirely by a protective coating of mucus, slide over thorns and gravel that would otherwise puncture their soft bodies. In the moist lowlands, where terrain permits the gathering of food and construction of shelters, raccoons and beavers can be found.

The brightly colored Steller's jay and the bold gray jay liven the forest with their raucous behavior. The hermit thrush, a seldom-seen denizen of the deep woods, makes its presence known with a haunting, slow, spiraling song.

Rare animals, like mountain lions and bobcats, visit this region briefly. Few and fortunate are those who have sighted them.

PAT O'HARA

Mushrooms abound following the warm rains of early fall.

The golden-mantled ground squirrel is a true hibernator.

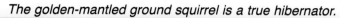

RALPH A. CLEVENGER

Dead snags provide convenient perches for predatory red-tailed hawks.

TOM & PAT LEESON

Active year-round, snowshoe hares are white in winter, brown in summer.

TOM & PAT LEESON

The bark and twigs of deciduous trees are the beaver's primary food source.

TOM & PAT LEESON

27

The glacial origin of Reflection Lakes is obscured by the forest. These lakes, along with nearby Lake Louise, lie in basins carved by glaciers.

THE SILVER FIR FOREST

The next major life zone, often known as the silver fir forest, is a checkered assortment of forest types dominated mostly by Pacific silver fir. This tree, a strong competitor, survives because of its ability to reproduce in its own shade and in the shade produced by other trees.

At the lower boundaries of this zone, around 2,200 feet, the silver fir often shares the forest floor with the noble fir, the largest of Mount Rainier's true firs. True firs have a dense, compact, often spiral-like crown. Their cones are borne upright and disintegrate at maturity, unlike the cones of the Douglas fir that hang downward and do not disintegrate. Western red cedar, western hemlock, and Douglas fir find the higher extremes of their range in the silver fir zone.

The silver fir zone yields an abundance of mouth-watering red and blue huckleberries, sought by both man and beast. When this region is in bloom, a variety of wildflowers show their color and form, from the urn-shaped fool's huckleberry to the solitary and exquisite rose-purple calypso orchid.

The upper reaches of the silver fir zone (4,500 feet) are dominated by yellow cedar, mountain hemlock, and silver fir. All these species suffer the rigors of altitude, high winds, drought, cold temperatures, wind-driven ice, and a short growing season: thus they are reduced in size. The yellow, or Alaska, cedar marks the transition to the next higher zone.

Throughout the silver fir forest, elk and black bears forage the open areas. Bears eat almost anything, although they are especially fond of huckleberries. Elk browse on twigs, bark, and shrubs. In summer the elk often abandon the silver fir forest for the high meadows and subalpine trees. Mountain goats wander through on their way to and from high summer meadows. In winter the goats sometimes remain in the silver fir forest.

Where stands of trees are separated by areas of rock, the "eek" of the pika may be heard as a ball of fur disappears down a rock crevice. The pika, a guinea pig–sized rodent, does not hibernate; it relies on stored food to survive through the winter. The pika stockpiles plant material by setting it out to dry in the summer sun, then storing it under rocks.

Identified as a true fir by its upright cones, the subalpine fir varies from a shrub at timberline to a 100-foot giant at lower elevations.

Several species of huckleberry can be found at Mount Rainier. The taste of the Cascades huckleberry, which ripens in September, is reflected in its species name, deliciosum.

The shade-tolerant western hemlock, which towers in majestic stands in the lowland forest, finds its upper range limit in the lower silver fir forest.

THE SUBALPINE

Above the forests stretches a mosaic of tree "islands" and meadows. The subalpine zone rises to the limits of the trees. Here, clusters of subalpine fir, silver fir, mountain hemlock, and yellow cedar create refuges against the elements. On the well-drained, ash-laden slopes of the mountain's east side, whitebark pine replaces mountain hemlock in isolated clumps. Lodgepole pine and Englemann spruce, which favor a drier climate, are occasionally found in the subalpine of the Sunrise area.

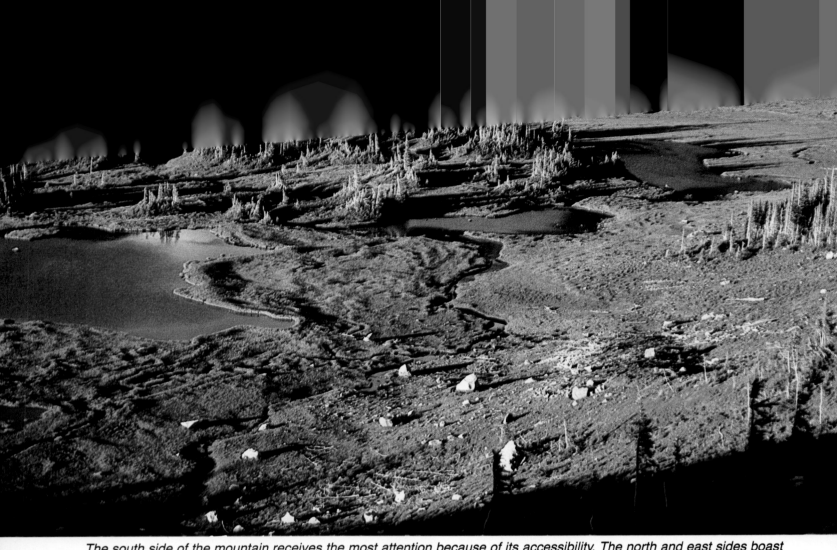

The south side of the mountain receives the most attention because of its accessibility. The north and east sides boast equally spectacular subalpine meadows, such as the Elysian Fields which can be reached by the Carbon River Trail.

During the September mating season, bull elk can sometimes be heard bugling on the park's east side.

Seedlings that stray too far from the protection and warmth of the dark, heat-absorbing adult trees soon die as winter winds sap life-giving moisture. The seedlings that sprout close to the warmth and shelter of the tree island have a better chance of surviving the rigors of winter, thus adding to the growth of the clump.

Subalpine fir does not reproduce solely by casting its seed to the unpredictable winds; it also sprouts roots and new growth where its branches touch the meadows. A single fir can create a clump of look-alikes, with younger trees often ringing the old and dying adult.

To survive the excessive weight of world-record snowfalls, the tree branches flex or shed the snow. The strong, rubbery limbs of whitebark pine bend under their load. The spearlike growths of subalpine fir shed the moisture-laden snow, which is so heavy and wet that it is often referred to as "Cascade cement."

At the upper limit of the subalpine zone, the severe climate and short growing season will not allow plants much woody growth. This border between the temperate forested region and a treeless alpine zone is strewn with trees scarred

K. C. DENDOOVEN

Almost any rock slope will shelter hoary marmots, which often signal their presence with a shrill whistle.

The white-tailed ptarmigan is well adapted to winter. It is camouflaged in white and has feathers on its feet, which act as snowshoes.

TOM & PAT LEESON

by the elements, living at their uppermost limit. Such trees are sensitive to the slightest variances in climate. Local conditions can keep trees from growing above 5,500 feet, or when favorable, allow them to survive as high as 6,500 feet. Such shifting limits of trees, or timberlines, are indicators of regional and global climatic trends.

Trees whose lower-slope relatives would be towering elsewhere, rarely exceed six or eight feet here. So marginal is their existence that they must grow as shrubs, with twisted branches pruned to bizarre shapes by wind-blown ice. Although their stature suggests youth, they are often ancient. Heat is in short supply, thus only a minuscule layer of wood can be added each growing season. Trees only inches in diameter can be as much as 250 years old!

The surrounding area of subalpine meadows is awash with some 20 feet of wind-sculptured snow more than six months of the year. In late July and August these meadows spring to life in a carpet of blossoms as colorful and varied as the most brilliant stained glass. Sky blue lupine, white avalanche lilies, yellow glacier lilies, magenta paintbrush, golden marsh marigolds, purple aster, and many others abound.

For the most part, the flowered parklands and tree clumps of the subalpine are home to the same creatures occupying lower elevations. The receding snows of summer allow elk to browse in high meadows, particularly in the north and east portions of the park.

Elk, which are not native to Mount Rainier, were introduced between 1912 and 1933 to areas near the park's boundaries. By 1934 the transplanted elk were invading the park to the detriment of the environment. The elk population continued to grow. What once were several small herds outside the park now is one herd of roughly 2,000 that resides in the park in summer.

Trampling and grazing by the herd has caused significant changes in the floral composition of subalpine meadows. Vegetation has been destroyed, trails have been eroded, and the watershed has been disrupted. The National Park Service, other concerned agencies, and citizen groups are continuing to study the problem to find an acceptable solution.

Black-tailed deer, black bears, and mountain goats also wander the subalpine meadows in search of summer food, shelter, and water. The hoary marmot, "groundhog of the west," eats huge quantities of greens and fruits in preparation for hibernation.

Hibernating animals burrow deeply for protection from the cold. The overlying snow, which can contain as much as 50 percent air, provides valuable insulation, keeping the animals' nests as warm as 45 degrees Fahrenheit while the temperature outside dips below freezing.

In this zone of diminishing trees and shrubs, protective coloration is crucial to the survival of animals not well equipped for fighting nor fleet of foot or wing. The chickenlike blue grouse blends in with the mottled background, drawing the attention of only the most observant. Often the first indication of its presence is its muffled, throaty call. At higher elevations the white-tailed ptarmigan, a small relative of the blue grouse, pecks about in the rocks and snow for insects and seeds. The ptarmigan changes its mottled summer plumage to pure white during winter.

With its strong legs and soft, slightly cupped hooves, the mountain goat is specially suited to life among rocky crags.

ALPINE

Above the tree line the landscape of rock appears sterile at a distance, but it is actually rich with uniquely adapted plants. The abundance of rock actually allows alpine plants to survive freezing summer temperatures and gale-force winds. In the comparatively warm, wind-protected lee of small stones, heather creeps outward, growing a quarter of an inch every ten years. Its evergreen leaves trap windblown soil, allowing more room for growth, yet burying the older part of the plant as new growth continues to push outward. The repeated growth, collection of soil, and subsequent burying can persist until the entire field of original stones is covered with stored soil. Some heather plants may have trapped soil for over 6,000 years, surviving periods of glaciation and catastrophic volcanic activity. If this cycle is totally disturbed, however, the entire store of soil can be swept away by wind and water, and heather growth must begin anew.

Higher fields of stones are colonized by plants like blue Lyall's lupine, the inconspicuous great alpine whitlow-grass, and the tightly tufted, slender polemonium. These plants also survive by growing in dense mats beside stones.

The permanent animal residents in the alpine zone are primarily deer mice, heather voles, spiders, and a few insects. Mountain goats may forage the area when the weather is warm. The high-spirited, gray-crowned rosy finch and the raven frequent summer climbing camps in search of food. They also venture onto snowfields to feast on windblown insects.

The animals and plants of high meadows carry an array of physical and chemical adaptations which enable them to survive. To reduce heat loss the mammals have round bodies with small ears, short legs, and little or no tail. The plants of these treeless neighborhoods, often only inches high, hug the ground for warmth and protection from wind. Each plant may have a taproot an inch in thickness, extending several feet deep and providing firm anchorage against wind as well as storing plentiful food for the long winter.

To combat excessive drying, the plants here often have small leaves. The leaves frequently grow in tight rosettes to capture the greatest amount of sunlight with the least exposure to cold. At the beginning and end of summer, the leaves and stems of many subalpine and alpine plants acquire a reddish tinge. The chemical responsible for this change can absorb solar energy to warm the plant tissue. These same leaves and stems may be covered with dense, woolly hairs to reflect excess solar radiation.

At about 9,000 feet weather extremes are too great for flowering plants. But in this world of perpetual snow and ice, the snow may be pink with algae and the most favorable rocks dotted with small circles of multicolored lichens. Conditions favorable to plant growth are so limited, and the pace of life is so slow, that a nickel-sized patch of lichen may be over 1,000 years old.

On the rock- and ice-choked landscape from 9,000 feet to the summit, one does not expect to encounter animal life. Yet reports of bears, deer mice, marmots, martens, and porcupines indicate that animals occasionally venture into this area. Why they do this, no one knows. Stranger still are the inch-long black ice worms that live year-round in alpine snowfields. These nocturnal relatives of the familiar earthworm thrive on algae. The worms are so well adapted to the cold that if they are kept at even 70 degrees Fahrenheit, they will overheat and die.

PLANT PIONEERS

Sweeping across the major zones of living organisms come snow avalanches, rock slides, floods, fires, and mudflows, destroying most vegetation in their paths. A variety of trees, shrubs, and weeds can reestablish a carpet of roots that has been severely disturbed or utterly destroyed by such natural disasters. These plants are the

Blue lupines and other wildflowers adorn the slopes of Paradise Valley. The shapes, colors, designs, and scents of these blossoms serve as lures, guides, and landing pads for pollinating insects.

pioneers. Their ability to persist in the poorest soil enables longer-lived plants, and the animals that go with them, to gain a foothold.

Pioneer plants do this by providing ground cover to lessen erosion and by returning organic material to the soil as they shed their leaves or die. Along avalanche paths and other areas where disturbances frequently recur, pioneers are the only plants able to survive, for the seedlings of less resilient plants are repeatedly stripped away.

In the aftermath of fire, the rosy spikes of fireweed soon return color to the land. In the wake of mudflow and flood, the red alder is quick to send down roots. But the most tenacious of pioneers seems to be the sitka alder. Its flexible form withstands snowy torrents in excess of 65 miles an hour.

Without these pioneer plants Mount Rainier would be barren and lifeless. Perhaps this is what the flower fields celebrate when they bloom in summer.

SUGGESTED READING

DEYRUP, MARK. "Deadwood Decomposers," *Natural History,* Vol. 90, p. 3, March 1981.

KOZLOFF, EUGENE N. *Plants and Animals of the Pacific Northwest.* Seattle: University of Washington Press, 1976.

LARRISON, EARL J., et al. *Washington Wildflowers.* Seattle: The Seattle Audubon Society, 1977.

MANNING, HARVEY. *Mountain Flowers.* Seattle: The Mountaineers, 1979.

McKENNY, MARGARET. *The Savory Wild Mushroom.* Revised and enlarged by Daniel E. Stuntz. Seattle: University of Washington Press, 1971.

MOSHER, MILTON M., and KNUT LUNNUM. *Trees of Washington.* Pullman: Washington State University, College of Agriculture, Cooperative Extension Service, Bulletin No. 440, 1974.

PYLE, ROBERT M. *Watching Washington Butterflies.* Seattle: Seattle Audubon Society, 1974.

SCHWARTZ, SUSAN. *Cascade Companion.* Seattle: Pacific Search Books, 1976.

ZWINGER, ANN H., and BEATRICE E. WILLARD. *Land Above the Trees: American Alpine Tundra.* New York: Harper, 1972.

Man at Mount Rainier

At least ten Native American tribes once lived in the shadow of Mount Rainier. They found a permanent place in their legends for the snowy dome that was inaccessible to them, at least most of the year. To these forest and grassland dwellers, the mountain had various meanings, including "running like thunder near the skies," "gives white to the land," and "breast of the milk-white waters."

Breathtaking views reward hikers a short distance from Paradise.

The legends were as colorful and varied as the landscape they described, yet most bore a hint of actual geological events that occurred in prehistoric times. A Chehalis Indian legend tells of two female mountains, Mount Rainier and Mount Saint Helens, quarreling over the male Mount Adams. The two women fought, throwing hot rocks and fire at each other until Mount Rainier was struck so hard that her head was broken off.

The Cowlitz Indians claimed Mount Rainier and Mount Adams as the women and Mount Saint Helens as the man, while the Nisqually held that Mount Rainier was a female monster who sucked all the people who came near her into her maw. Mount Rainier was defeated by the "Changer," in the form of a fox, in a contest to see who could suck in the most people. Mount Rainier died and streams of blood ran down her sides. The Changer transformed the blood into water that still flows down the mountain's slopes as rivers and creeks. The Cowlitz River, Olallie Creek, Mowich Lake, and Wauhaukaupauken Falls are but a few of these places that still bear Indian names.

Considering these legends, as well as the scant artifacts that have turned up, archaeologists believe that tools and other evidence at least 8,000 years old could remain hidden in the park. If so, such material must endure the test of time in a landscape smothered with vegetation, torn by violent change, and pitted by constant erosion. Archaeologists theorize that stone tools, charred wood, and other evidence unearthed so far hint at, but do not confirm, human use prior to 6,000 years ago.

Native Americans were drawn to the lower reaches of Mount Rainier. Here, in a land nurtured by volcanic rock and ash, they found food and raw materials for clothing and tools. In the spring they climbed the slopes as the snow melted, retreating as winter returned. Their forays to the mountain were only for sustenance, however.

These people and their descendants later guided the curious white men who came with eyes fixed on Rainier's summit.

Since 1912 skiers have been drawn to the slopes of Mount Rainier.

From the northwest

Mount Rainier

The many moods of Mount Rainier can be captured along the park's excellent road and trail system. Serene, somber, threatening, or majestic, the mountain dominates the scene.

Photos by Ed Cooper

From the west

From the southwest

From the north

From the northeast

From the east

From the south

From the southeast

EXPLORATION AND EXPLOITATION

In 1792 Captain George Vancouver, a British explorer, became the first European to gaze across Puget Sound and make note of Mount Rainier. Vancouver named it after his friend Rear Admiral Peter Rainier, in keeping with the custom of the times.

William Fraser Tolmie, a capable young Scot who practiced medicine at Fort Nisqually, employed five Indians as guides on a botanical excursion toward Mount Rainier in 1833. In his efforts to collect medicinal herbs, Tolmie became the first white man to enter what is now Mount Rainier National Park.

In both historic and legendary times, accounts existed of Indians successfully climbing Mount Rainier. The validity of such accounts is perhaps a matter of faith and will always remain uncertain. Historical records of early climbs by white men are likewise scant.

In 1857 a well-documented attempt to climb Mount Rainier was made by August Valentine Kautz, an Army lieutenant at nearby Fort Steilacoom. Kautz lived with the mountain practically in his backyard and soon developed an immense desire to reach its summit. He and his companions employed a Nisqually Indian, Wahpowety, as a guide. In July they headed for the foot of the Nisqually Glacier.

After six days of travel through forest and thicket, they began to climb. By the eighth day Kautz's guide was suffering from snow blindness and his companions gave out behind him. But Kautz probably reached the 14,000-foot level, some 400 feet shy of the summit. Although he was greatly disappointed, Kautz had proved that the Northwest's greatest mountain could be climbed.

While Mount Rainier remained unconquered, the profile of the mountain from afar was gaining notoriety. As settlements spread along the seacoast, the need for more precise landmarks became apparent, so a U.S. naval squadron set about mapping the coastline. They chose Mount Rainier as a landmark, giving it an altitude of 12,330 feet. Even at this reduced stature—today it is considered to be 14,410 feet high—the summit remained unchallenged.

In the two years that followed Kautz's attempt, James Longmire, a settler from Indiana who had a farm south of Fort Steilacoom, established a route from the coast to the inclines of Mount Rainier. Known as the Packwood Trail, the rough byway became the path of would-be climbers. Longmire became the guide.

The Kautz Icefall, consisting of narrow terraces and slippery ice pinnacles, requires technical mountaineering skills to negotiate. Lieutenant August Kautz, the first to prove that Mount Rainier could be climbed, passed this spot in 1857. He made his approach from the steep snowfields above Van Trump Park. Captain George Vancouver, however, was responsible for naming Mount Rainier. His choice of names later precipitated considerable argument. Some preferred an Indian name, Tahoma or Tacoma, instead of Mount Rainier.

The old Longmire homestead is a quiet, secluded site near contemporary Longmire. The Trail of the Shadows takes visitors past mineral springs—the original site of the Longmire Springs Hotel, a beaver dam, and this cabin built about 1888 by James Longmire's son Elcaine.

ED COOPER

Eleven years later a trio of determined climbers from Olympia were guided by Longmire to the end of the Packwood Trail. Here, three miles south of the community of Longmire, Hazard Stevens, Philemon Van Trump, and Edmund T. Coleman hired the Yakima Indian, Sluiskin, as their guide to the snow line.

Coleman soon dropped out, unable to continue. At what is now called Sluiskin Falls, Sluiskin eloquently warned the remaining two men of the dangers of the ice-clad slopes above:

> Your plan to climb Takhoma is all foolishness. . . . At first the way is easy, the task seems light. The broad snowfields over which I have hunted the mountain goat offer an inviting path. But above them you will have to climb over steep rocks overhanging deep gorges. . . . And if you reach the great snowy dome, then a bitterly cold and furious tempest will sweep you off into space like a withered leaf. . . .

They were undaunted, and on August 17, 1870, after ten and a half hours of climbing, the pair stood on Mount Rainier's highest point. Darkness was soon upon them, and with it, an approaching storm. Lacking shelter, they were forced to spend an uncomfortable night on the summit huddled in the mouth of an ice cavern hollowed and warmed by volcanic steam. Stevens and Van Trump left a brass nameplate and a canteen on the summit to document the first successful ascent. Their adventure sparked an interest in climbing that to this day has not subsided.

Having lived under the pull of the mountain for some time, James Longmire finally challenged the icy grandeur, yielding to the prodding of friends. In 1883, when he was 63, Longmire climbed the mountain for the first time. On the way, he camped near several soda and iron springs. Longmire saw these springs as an economic opportunity. Later he established Mount Rainier's first hotel at the site—a move that was instrumental in publicizing the natural wonders of the region. Touting the medicinal value of the spring water and mineral baths as a cure-all, his advertisements reached far and wide. But those who came were just as likely to be soothed by the spring's surroundings as they were by the waters themselves.

John Muir came not for cures, but for horses. In 1888 when Muir rented horses from Longmire, he wrote his wife that he had not meant to climb the mountain, "but got excited and soon was on top." Such was the manner in which the articulate 50-year-old conservationist found himself upon the summit in the company of photographer Arthur C. Warner. With the writings of Muir and

the pictures of young Warner, the American people became familiar with the grandeur of Mount Rainier.

The mountain began to enjoy what would become a century of influence on American mountaineering. Mount Rainier's climbing history continued to be made. In 1890 Fay Fuller, a Tacoma schoolteacher, became the first woman to reach the summit. Led by Longmire's son Len, Fuller was properly attired in sun hat and long woolen skirt.

The early explorers and climbers were uncommon men and women of great achievement and determination. More often than not their equipment amounted to no more than a suit of woolen clothes, a blanket, and nails pounded through the soles of their shoes. Mount Rainier continued to be a magnet to those wanting to climb snow and ice at high altitudes.

For 20 years after Fay Fuller's ascent, Len

Mount Rainier is often obscured by lingering cloud banks. At such times the wonders close at hand are worth contemplating.

RAY ATKESON

Longmire continued to acquaint people with Mount Rainier, guiding them from Camp Muir to the summit for a dollar. Fay Fuller also continued to climb the mountain, recounting its climbing history and stressing in articles published in her father's newspaper the need for making the mountain a national park.

The camaraderie on the alpine slopes resulted in the organization of mountaineering clubs along the Pacific Coast. In 1897 the Mazamas, a newly formed group destined to become a leading contemporary mountaineering organization, herded over 200 of its members along rough trails from Portland, Oregon, to Paradise Valley. The largest party to assemble on the mountain to date, they arrived with 45 tents, 4 tons of supplies, 2 beef steers, 7 milk cows, and many horses. Fifty-eight reached the summit and fired off red flares in celebration, delighting Tacoma, Washington, residents.

Despite its increasing popularity, the mountain remained unforgiving. Early climbing history is replete with tales of discomfort, bruised bodies, breathtaking slides, and in 1897, the first recorded climbing fatality. Since that time over 50 lives have been lost.

In the late nineteenth century, railroad companies publicized the natural wonders of the Far West. Company representatives often returned from Mount Rainier expressing hopes that the mountain would soon become a national park. After all, it was good business. The culmination of this increasing interest came on March 2, 1899, when President McKinley signed the act establishing Mount Rainier as the nation's fifth national park.

A Mountain Playground

With the advertising of Longmire Medical Springs, the park grew steadily in popularity. Also, tent camps that sprang up in Paradise Valley received considerable publicity. These camps were owned by businessmen and provided tourists with room and board for as little as three dollars a day. One spot, sometimes called Camp of the Clouds, became the starting point for nearly all summit climbers and day hikers.

At the dawn of a new century, Paradise Valley was not only the established hub of climbing

DAVID MUENCH

Even in summer, snow lingers in the high country. As a result, areas such as Frozen Lake are accessible for only a few months each year.

within the new national park, but was also the center of Pacific Northwest mountaineering and a mecca for climbers from Europe.

Horse-drawn stages carrying regular visitors found the toll road up the Nisqually Valley—the only way of reaching the park—treacherous, rough, and muddy. Visiting the remote park required an adventurous spirit and several days of travel. In 1904 the Tacoma and Eastern Railroad constructed a line to Ashford, six miles short of the park boundary. This smoothed the way to Mount Rainier, but the best of horse-drawn rigs still required four and a half hours to travel the last ten miles to the Longmire Springs Hotel.

D. C. LOWE/APERTURE

Surrounded by Yakima Peak's subalpine meadows, Tipsoo Lake is a popular attraction in summer. Meadow flowers are at their colorful peak during the few snow-free weeks, but winter is always around the corner, and blizzards may come even in July. Although many areas are easily accessible in summer, winter snowstorms can last for days, rendering much of the park inaccessible to all but properly skilled and equipped travelers.

PAT O'HARA

The park administration and the U.S. Army Corps of Engineers hired Eugene Ricksecker, a remarkable civilian engineer, to design and build a suitable road from the park's entrance to Paradise. Ricksecker strove to preserve the scenic beauty of the forested valley through which the highway would pass. When completed, the road struck a splendid balance between engineering principles and landscape preservation.

In anticipation of improved access to the park, the Tacoma and Eastern Railroad constructed the National Park Inn adjacent to the Longmire Springs Hotel. At these rustic hostelries tourists dined and rested for less than four dollars a day. Both establishments enjoyed good business. Most of the National Park Inn burned down in 1926, leaving only the two-story annex built in 1916. Now known as the National Park Inn, the annex still provides accommodations for visitors.

In 1908 an improved highway was opened to the public as far as the Nisqually Glacier. In a nation that was marveling almost daily at ex-

ceptional engineering feats, the people of the Northwest, along with the park superintendent, boasted with understandable pride about the "first road constructed by the United States to reach a glacier." (At that time, the Nisqually Glacier was about 1,700 feet from the highway bridge, compared to over a mile today.) Although horses still had the right of way at all times, automobiles sped toward the new wonders at speeds of up to 15 miles an hour.

In the fall of 1911 the first automobile sputtered toward Paradise over a rough and muddy track, with President William H. Taft as a passenger. His horseless carriage had to be towed by

The trail to Plummer Peak is just one of over 300 miles of trails providing backcountry access.

horses for the latter part of the journey. Improvements in road construction were swift, however, and a year later an automobile operating under its own power reached Paradise Valley.

In 1915, with an awkward system of traffic control, the highway from Nisqually Glacier to Paradise, often only ten feet wide, was opened to one-way public auto travel.

Although much of Mount Rainier's colorful and event-filled history occurred after 1915, nothing had such a far-reaching and lasting effect as the arrival of automobiles at Paradise. With them came improved facilities and new services. Since 1917 the Paradise Inn has provided lodging for people from all walks of life. Among them were such notables as Sonja Heine, Shirley Temple, Tyrone Power, Cecil B. De Mille, and the crown prince of Norway. In 1918 a public auto campground was constructed at Longmire. Today, six campgrounds give visitors an inexpensive choice of accommodations in the park.

Park highways have continued to improve over the years. Travelers can now reach Mount Rainier's west, south, and east flanks during the summer. Among these routes is the spectacular road to Sunrise, terminating at 6,500 feet—the highest point in the park attainable by car.

A variety of edible wild berries, including salmonberries, thimbleberries, and red and blue huckleberries, are sought by both man and beast.

What appears from a distance to be level glacial terrain is actually broken by enormous blocks of ice called seracs and by deep chasms.

In addition to the new roads, a trail system encircling the mountain was completed in 1916. This system opened the park to tourists and allowed for efficient patrolling by rangers. Known today as the Wonderland Trail, this 95-mile path crosses snowfields, skirts glaciers, spans countless streams, descends to lowland forest valleys, and climbs to ridge tops well above the timberline.

Even though stimulated by rapid turn-of-the-century progress and tireless promoters, some developments, events, and services declined in later years because of changing attitudes and economics. It became apparent that some activities were threatening Mount Rainier's natural resources and wilderness character.

Gone from Paradise Valley are an unsuccessful nine-hole golf course and a motorcycle hill climb whose hillside scars became too noticeable. Rented boats once plied the waters of Reflection Lake, and an Eskimo and dog team offered sled rides for a fee until feeding the dogs became too expensive.

The slopes above Paradise no longer have any ski lifts, jumps, or races. Contestants used to race from Camp Muir to Paradise Valley, an event heralded in the 1930s as the "wildest annual ski race on the North American continent." The trip covered four miles and over 4,500 feet of elevation.

In the 1930s the increasing popularity of Mount Rainier had taken its toll on the park's roads, trails, and facilities. As a result, badly needed renovations were completed by the Civilian Conservation Corps. Numerous buildings, trails, rock walls, and bridges were built that are still in service today.

Since the 1930s the popularity of Mount Rainier has not decreased. Once again visitor facilities and historic structures are in need of major rehabilitation. At present the National Park Service is renovating and restoring visitor facilities and historic buildings. This is just one of many programs at Mount Rainier that allow people to use and enjoy the park in a way that will enable future generations to enjoy it as well.

Thousands of people climb Mount Rainier each year. Some days, over 100 climbers register at the summit. Hazardous terrain and severe weather require that climbers have a basic knowledge of mountain and glacier travel. A climb can involve a gain of more than 9,000 feet over a distance of only eight miles or so. Normal summer climbing time from Camp Muir is about 12 hours round trip. Physical conditioning can offset the effects of fatigue and altitude that often lead to accidents.

The mountain holds many challenges for the experienced technical climber. The more popular climbing routes demand more physical effort than advanced ability.

Camp Muir, at 10,000 feet, is four miles from Paradise. The hike takes up to six hours.

SUGGESTED READING

CLARK, ELLA E. *Indian Legends of the Pacific Northwest.* Berkeley: University of California Press, 1971.

FERBER, PEGGY, Ed. *Mountaineering: The Freedom of the Hills.* Seattle: The Mountaineers, 1974.

HAINES, AUBREY L. *Mountain Fever, Historic Conquest of Rainier.* Portland: Oregon Historical Society, 1962.

KIRK, RUTH. *Exploring Mount Rainier.* Seattle: University of Washington Press, 1968.

MANNING, HARVEY, and IRA SPRING. *Fifty Hikes in Mount Rainier National Park. 3d ed.* Seattle: The Mountaineers, 1988.

MOLENAAR, DEE. *The Challenge of Rainier.* Seattle: The Mountaineers, 1979.

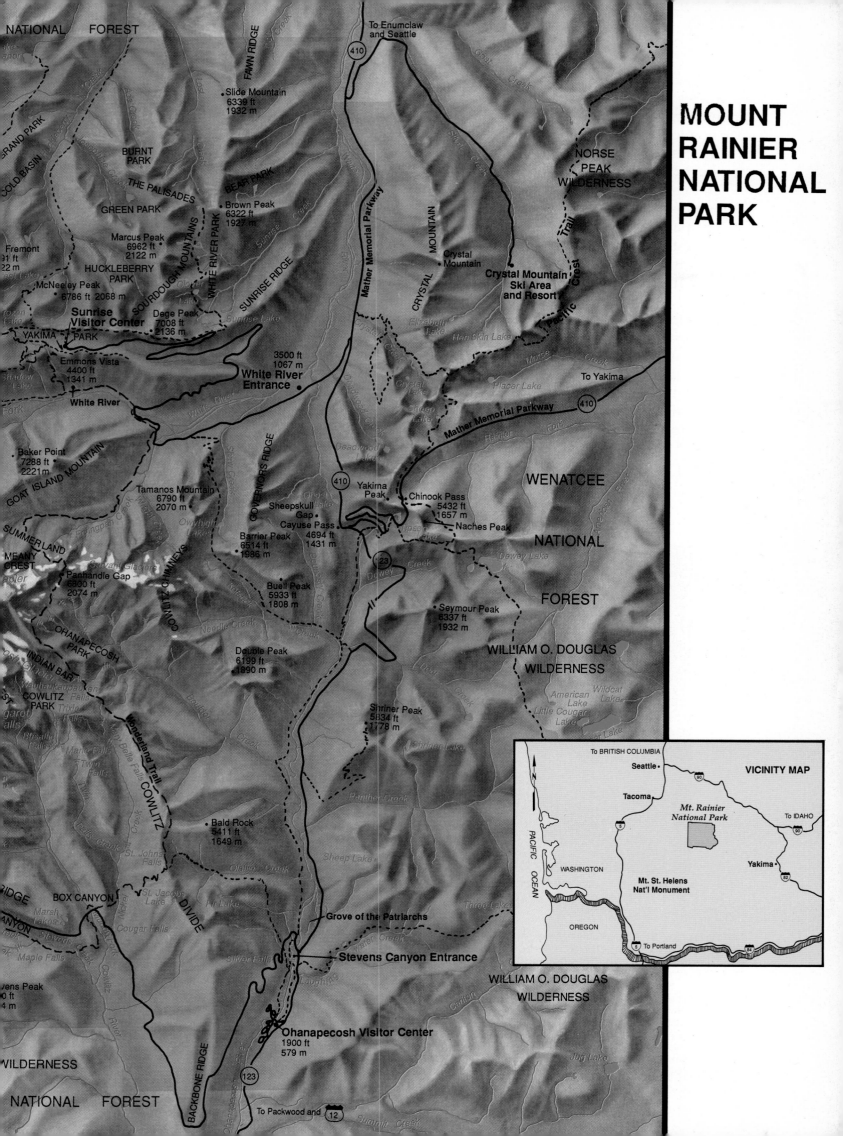

Mount Rainier Today

Night does not fall on the shoulders of Mount Rainier. It rises from the valley floors and clefts of the mountains, smudging timberlines and contours of rock and ice cliffs. It rises to cloud the ridge tops in dark blue-green velvet and reaches to join the rosy hues of alpenglow.

To experience Mount Rainier is to encounter the moods and challenges of the Northwest's greatest. The park itself encompasses 235,612 acres of mostly untrammeled wilderness. Experiences at the mountain take many forms, but most of us return with the same reward—a sense of self-renewal.

Admiration is often contagious, however, and the heralding of Mount Rainier's charms has been widespread. Ever-increasing numbers of visitors are taking advantage of the abundant recreational opportunities, creating a plethora of challenging resource management problems. What steps must be taken to protect the hikers' experience as well as the land they walk? And how do you ensure the well-being of mountain wildflowers when thousands of summer visitors step from their cars to join the confusion of color and fragrance? These and other management concerns require thoughtful and innovative solutions.

The challenges are being met. Park rangers help visitors plan safe and enjoyable trips into the backcountry, and inform them how to keep the impact of hiking and camping to a minimum. Attractive trailhead exhibits and park foot patrols advise of the need to stay on established paths while in the wildflower meadows.

The future of Mount Rainier is ensured by a mandate that directs the National Park Service to provide for the public's enjoyment of the park's spectacular scenery, but only in a manner that will leave it unimpaired for the enjoyment of new generations.

The resources of Mount Rainier remain essentially unspoiled as a direct result of public interest. "The Mountain" deserves to be cared for and managed on a par with the love that the people of the Northwest and the rest of the nation have for it. That calls for a great deal of care indeed.

CORDY & JUDY WAGNER

Spectacular skies may include cloudcaps, wave clouds, and sun shadows.

The mountain continually challenges our perceptions of scale and distance.

Back cover: Mount Rainier offers solitude and self-renewal.
Photos by David Muench

Books in the Story Behind the Scenery series: Acadia, Alcatraz Island, Arches, Blue Ridge Parkway, Bryce Canyon, Canyon de Chelly, Canyonlands, Cape Cod, Capitol Reef, Channel Islands, Civil War Parks, Colonial, Crater Lake, Death Valley, Denali, Dinosaur, Everglades, Fort Clatsop, Gettysburg, Glacier, Glen Canyon-Lake Powell, Grand Canyon, Grand Canyon-North Rim, Grand Teton, Great Smoky Mountains, Haleakala, Hawaii Volcanoes, Independence, Lake Mead-Hoover Dam, Lassen Volcanic, Lincoln Parks, Mount Rainier, Mount Rushmore, Mount St. Helens, National Park Service, National Seashores, North Cascades, Olympic, Petrified Forest, Redwood, Rocky Mountain, Scotty's Castle, Sequoia-Kings Canyon, Shenandoah, Statue of Liberty, Theodore Roosevelt, Virgin Islands, Yellowstone, Yosemite, Zion.
NEW: in pictures — The Continuing Story: Bryce Canyon, Death Valley, Everglades, Grand Canyon, Sequoia-Kings Canyon, Yellowstone, Zion.

Published by KC Publications · Box 14883 · Las Vegas, NV 89114

Printed by Dong-A Printing and Publishing, Seoul, Korea
Separations by Color Masters